M000201660

Selected Poems

William Greenway

FUTURECYCLE PRESS
www.futurecycle.org

Published by FutureCycle Press
Hayesville, North Carolina, USA

ISBN 978-1-938853-50-0

For Elton, *il miglior fabbro*

Contents

From
PRESSURE UNDER GRACE

From
WHERE WE'VE BEEN

From
HOW THE DEAD BURY THE DEAD

From
SIMMER DIM

From
ASCENDING ORDER

From
FISHING AT THE END OF THE WORLD

From
EVERYWHERE AT ONCE

From
PRESSURE UNDER GRACE

Breitenbush Books, 1982

The Fortune

You will go on a long journey:
the land is covered with gray clouds,
the earth impeccably carpeted
with dead grass.
The friends you leave behind will change
or die,
and letters will grow fewer.
The distant winter trees
will grow in the mist
like gray wool touched with rust.
You will acquire money,
but not enough;
you will acquire fame,
but not enough;
you will have love;
it will be too much
until it is not enough.
You will end alone
far from any light
on a country road at night.
You will meet a tall, dark stranger.

Heir Apparent

One of my grandfathers was a Georgia
butcher
who beat *niggers* and my mother,
drank moonshine from a paper bag,
and told me
If you ever squat to pee,
you and me are through.

The other
was a Welsh preacher
with long, delicate fingers
who sang *Oh*
What a Beautiful Morning
the day his son wed
the Georgia butcher's girl.

They are both here
and they are both dead
sometimes late at night,
hands on hips on either
side of me,
two giants, each
glaring, defying the other,
while I tremble between.

My Father's House

Every Sunday, over cheap tar roads,
caving at the shoulders,
snaking through ruined forests,
we went looking for new houses
in the child-empty suburbs,
miles on yellow buses
from any school.
The lumber and sawdust yards
were red wounds or craters
filled with sand, bent nails, and half bricks,
needle-shaded by thin pines.

Hollow, each house smelled of raw wood;
each room echoed with our voices.
We walked paper aisles across floors
dusted with fine wood talcum.
In the kitchens without water or light,
over sinks full of dead wasps,
we looked at the view:
endless pines full of purple shadow, framed
by unfinished plaster, molding never
quite meeting, and paint
dribbled on the light switches.
We brought our old furniture inside
with us, in our minds,
and pushed it into corners to see
if it would fit,
could look better there.

And when we thought it did,
we bought them and moved in,
brought our clothes, records,
boxes of books and china,
into those houses, already empty,
haunted.

William Greenway | 13

The House on the Second Floor

I have been half in love with easeful Death.
—Keats

I see the seasons change
through the window glazed
with white gauze curtains,
which breathe in the long afternoons
of summer, wash the winter tree,
bring flaring red autumn in,
and green spring,
one shade pale.

On this back street
there is no noise; steps
of the occasional old man
going for groceries
are muffled on the mossy walks.
I see him without parting
the curtains, but he cannot see me.

I sit and look down
at their life in a quiet neighborhood
while spirits,
like whispers almost palpable,
move through the high empty rooms
and glide by mirrors hung
just past the corners of my eyes.

These ghosts I have grown used to,
and they to me; they love the living company,
and I love their awe
as they pass, hushed in wonder at one
not lost into the stillness at the last,
but coming early on—
exploring.

The Night Before I Left

Scared, my suitcase locked on the bed,
I walked downstairs
to tell him.
Down all three levels I moved
through all the things he'd earned
to find him in the den alone, the lights off,
drinking a diet cola and bourbon,
watching the late movie.

My lips trembling,
I sat down near him and started to speak,
when he leaned up and touched my arm, saying,
This is the good part coming up,
where these natives in New Guinea think...
the first time they saw an airplane,
they thought it was God.
They think an airplane is God.

I still see him, bending to the screen,
hair white, his glasses silver globes
crossed by black clouds,
watching natives once again
dig a tiny runway of dirt,
build a tower of sticks,
then sit down on their heels
in the dust to watch the sky and wait
the way their fathers did
and their fathers before them.

From
WHERE WE'VE BEEN

Breitenbush Books, 1987

Heart

He tells me I'm a risk:
he is small, blond, Mississippian. I trust him.
I am fighting my genes, he says, fighting
my father at fifty-six pulling off the highway
that had become a gray blur,
trying to call to anyone from a phone booth
while it broke in his chest, calcified, knobby
like an anklebone,
and then again, over and over
in the hospital while doctors
ran up and down the halls trying to stop
that sequence of explosions,
that string of firecrackers.

You see yourself as glass
for the first time, transparent,
shaken and fizzing, and start
watching for potholes.
Or maybe you just learn to live
with a cart with square wheels
thudding in your breast,
trying to carry whatever it is
there,
before it's too late.

This is how to become
old—worry only
about yourself,
so that if there come
bombs out of clouds
or lovers into rooms, saying
goodbyes, learn
to cup your hand around it,
as if, in a world of wind,
there is this one candle
that must be saved.

The Unities on North Avenue

I pried them from baseball
bats, made them learn my
lines, sell tickets,
and we swept the red
dirt of our dank
cellar, strung a curtain
(shower), lit stolen
candles, called it
a tragedy.

Somewhere, halfway through,
the plot began to improvise
itself, a flock of script taking
wing, the spear (rake)
used on the wrong end.
A wooden sword cleft
the gray loaf of yellow
jackets who descended like
critics; the plastic curtain
sizzled black fog.

As I rounded the dogwood,
mother after me
with the rake/spear, I looked
back and decided to go
into poetry:
a frieze, a tableau—Jimmy
Jacobs, his cape a still-
attached and whirling
muleta to Poochie
the dog, had delicate
blond Joe Nelson, who would
die at ten, in a headlock,
the basement behind spewing
ash and smoke, a sacked
city, bees swirling
around them like golden
snow in a crystal ball.

Double Feature

Tonight they're running it again:
I ran in the backyard for days yelling
Shane! Come back Shane! after I
saw it, and just remembered where:
we'd leave the house to get there
before dark, cool at night in the summer,
and I cried quietly, mosquitoes and voices
in the back seat with me,
where I saw *The Thing,*
huge and strong, vegetable, almost
unkillable.

Those were the good old days before
I got disconnected, like Alan Ladd only
far less fast or blond,
more like James Arness, stranded and vicious,
bleeding dust when cut.

He wore a buckskin shirt and went
away because he loved his best friend's
wife. When they found him
under the ice, my hair
rose as they held hands and spread
out across the snow, making a hushed
circle of that shape, everything
I ever wanted to be inside.

The Life of the Mind

My, my. A body does get around.
—Lena Grove

The summer Del
Shannon had a hit with "Runaway"
I was failing algebra, and my
grandfather told the story about slugging
his English teacher, jumping out
the window to run away and work
for the railroad, and eventually have mother
who had me.

Clark Goswick and I, on the last
day of school, before report cards
came in the mail, left
for Daytona Beach
to work on fishing boats and marry
Cuban girls, but a cop caught us
after only two miles and four hours.
As we walked up the driveway, bleeding, our backpacks
solid with canned beans and bristling
with fishing rods, mother called
from the porch,
Did they let school out early?

When I fall across my desk,
stricken, teaching
"The Road Not Taken" for the thousandth time,
an old salt on a dock somewhere
in Florida will be splicing
rope and telling yarns
to the dark children
of children.

Men as Trees, Walking

I learned early what that verse
meant, *For now we see as through a glass
darkly.* My mother wouldn't buy me any
glasses because then I'd be a four-eyes,
maybe even play in the band like the rest
of the pansies, or like my father, polishing
his lenses, head bent, hands
before his face as if praying,
no football hero.
Teachers tired of my leaning
in from the front row, chalk dust in
my hair, begged her in notes: like the blind
man in the Bible miracle, he sees men
as trees, and trees as lime
Jell-O.
Going out for passes, I was
lost like the end of the world when
everybody running sees the sky but me.
The coach threw his hat in the dust, *Son,
have you **ever** caught a pass?* I never
did, but when she gave in, let me have
my specs, it was like heaven, she even more
beautiful with wrinkles, people gross
as bears now limber as hickory, spare
as willows. And the trees, firmed up,
erect at last, were like emerald fish
with each scale whole and succinct,
as if they would never ever drop a leaf
or a pass.

Milledgeville

Castles of red brick in the rain, where my
"Granny" was, who thought jets flew over
to take pictures of her clothesline of old panties.
Things she said made the newspapers: *There,*
she'd say, triumphant, *I told you they*
were listening. From the fireplace.
She could stay there till death,
or they could cut, a fifty-
fifty chance, the first one.
Downstairs at night my father shouted
against his sisters. *Be it on your*
head, then, they said.

He took us to see her, maybe the last
time, walking into old light
like yellow dust, lampshades, cracked green
walls, a room of sofas and steel bars.
She cried and called him Billy, a child.
Take me home. I looked just
like him, her Billy. She wore a flimsy
flower print, for Sunday, black shoes
like a witch's, pointed bun of white hair.
Somewhere way off inside
there was groaning, other crying.

Your parents always said, *If you don't behave*
we'll send you to Milledgeville. Now I know
it was a real town, where Flannery O'Connor
lived with her mother and peacocks that called
like souls at dusk, remember how we left her
sobbing out *lobotomy* all the way back down
the hall, and the next day, how it showed up
in all the papers.

Pit Pony

There are only a few left, he says—
kept by old Welsh miners, souvenirs,
like gallstones or gold teeth, torn
from this "pit," so cold and wet
my breath comes out a soul up
into my helmet's lantern beam,
anthracite walls running, gleaming,
and the floors iron-rutted with tram tracks,
the almost pure rust that grows and waves
like orange moss in the gutters of water
that used to rise and drown.
He makes us turn all lights off, almost
a mile down. While children scream,
I try to see anything, my hand touching
my nose, my wife beside me—darkness
palpable, like a velvet sack over our heads,
even the glow of watches left behind.
This is where they were born, into
this nothing, felt first with their cold noses
for the shaggy side and warm bag of black milk,
pulled their trams for twenty years
through pitch, past birds that didn't sing,
through doors opened by five-year-olds
who sat in the cheap, complete blackness
listening for steps, a knock.
And they died down here, generation
after generation.
The last one, when it dies in the hills,
not quite blind, the mines closed forever,
will it die strangely? Will it wonder
dimly why it was exiled from the rest
of its race, from the dark flanks of the soft
mother, what these timbers are that hold up
nothing but blue? If this is the beginning
of death, this wind, these stars?

A1A

When we hit that highway in Jacksonville,
a veil parted into an otherness five hundred
miles and ten days from August's red
dirt, scrub pine, and football
practice, where my mother wanted
an athlete, and the coach wanted a state
championship. Skinny, timid,
I just wanted a stay of execution,
mixed of crushed bleached shells
and tar, blown and puddled with white
sand, running all the way down the coast just
behind one long dune, a green rampart
of sea oats and Spanish bayonet, Florida's
groves of water oak and olive even
at noon black, clustered, gnarled
Greek women whispering together, shade
caves of rusted cutlasses, eye patches, pieces
of eight falling spangled through twigs
onto the rooted gray sand carpeted with brown
scalloped leaves.
Fronds rattled all night in the salt wind,
and neon palms blinked red, green
red, green. Motels, Moorish, Tahitian, flashed
Vacancy, their hula girls flickering hips back
and forth, the boardwalk over the beach
pouring pastel cotton candy, apple smells
and the heavy oil of hamburgers, onions,
corn dogs, boiled crabs. The screaming rides,
calliopes, drowned the hissing of the surf.
Every morning we drove, our car full
of coffee steam and canned milk, to the pier
stilted out over the green waves, its boards
strewn with translucent pink confetti, bits,
baby fingernails of shrimp shell and fish scale,
cobbles of lead sinkers crusted white with salt, snarled

blond nests of old nylon line. We never caught
much, but the whole ocean was always there
in case. And the fishing camp, muffled with stained
sawdust, where we watched the throbbing boats
come in, throw colored bowed fish, sliding
in ice slime, onto the dock, a shark
hanging on a hook, its gray bark
I reached out to touch with one finger,
a dark deep-sea pool with fins
gliding, giant turtle that raised its beaked
head to *pshaw* spray into the warm air above
where we walked across a wooden bridge, afraid
we were falling through the cracks. It was
always there, summer after summer the
same until that last year, riding in on the first
day, there all along, one thing too
many, a field bulldozed free
of palms and palmetto, where they practiced
football, the year I noticed that the blue
scrolled sign of our motel the Shangra La
was spelled without an "i."

A Cat in Eden

They make fun of our spoiling her, felt
catnip toys, canned escargot, a tiny
wine list.
But her forerunner got hit chasing
squirrels in the street because we wanted her
to be free, happy, the one we raised
by hand with a doll's bottle she sucked
and chewed, her blind mouth brimming
with evaporated milk. She made a nest
in my hair at night, and I had fleas
for months, long after she was dead.

This one wears a harness and leash
she drags around the yard all day
like a small, abandoned sled dog.
Most of the time she just sits, miserable,
humiliated, as if she's being forced to wear
a hat. We keep a broomstick
handy for dogs and snakes.

They only live ten or twelve years
anyway, at the most,
but we want to bury her wrinkled
arthritic, bored,
though she sits for hours thinking, scheming
of a breakout, dreaming
of mice and trashcans,
hating our guts.

We could care less: we don't
philosophize
anymore—we just
patrol.

Karma

In my other life, I stayed
up all night, in charge of the moon
in the clearing, where the sticks
got up and
joined hands and
danced.
I had a crown of clover and baby's breath
and sweet minions
and I presided sitting on a soft
mushroom, drinking moonshine
from an acorn cup till dawn
when I was put to snore between the roots
of a great tree.
This went on for three hundred years
and I died.

I woke up human, and Baptist, in Atlanta, Georgia—
which shows you what can happen
when you don't pay attention.

Visitation

I'd been there before, knew when I stepped
off the plane, a hick, into the air-conditioned
air. There was smog, yes, but something
else, a tang—eucalyptus, burning
brush in the sun, a cool musk blowing
off a northern sea that the folds of the desert
hills poured into, congealed like lava.
The freeways, bald and ugly, rolled themselves
by blue waves flecked with the jade pods
of kelp, cold brine and a beach
the color of flesh. At evening crepe
myrtle, mimosa, hibiscus, frangipani trailed
tentacles, scarlet cupped, and the scent of warm
sage, shades of conquistadors in pewter,
boulevards of heron-crested palms leaned
in, all my movies, Saturday matinees, confused:
Tom Mix zinging bullets off of boulders just
over the hill from the beast with a million
eyes, giant ants and the San Andreas
fault, a lavender stain of sand sliding
quietly south by San Jacinto like a mountain
of the moon. The radio sifted the air
for a song, "Riders On the Storm," the notes
flickering stars above Mount Palomar,
a crowd with candles shouting *jump*
to someone on a ledge, white-robed
congregations at night in blind canyons, lights
of L.A., a pond of phosphorescent motes seen
from mountains of coyotes, howling.
I told no one my vision—the earth, dirty,
dangerous and holy—except once:
a group laughing on the beach,
brown, oily and floured with sand.
They loved my accent and made me say it over
and over, like a cowboy star of the thirties
or something from another world.

The Weaning

It starts with little things—
a blue web belt from the Navy,
a book of the greatest chess games,
a boy scout knife with ten blades.
You suspect that this time
they have not been lost, or mislaid, or left somewhere,
but subtracted,
that something has begun
erasing,
like ciphers, like tracks,
the curios of your history
starting back at the first
and gaining on you every day.
When you begin to miss certain people,
you know the house itself is next
or the street of green trees.
One morning when you wake it will be
color
and you will wander for days in snow
before, suddenly, even the whiteness goes.
But by then it will be
just one more thing.

It's What You Said You Wanted

My old fishing buddy calls to ask
if I still want that skull, that a guy's
in town selling them at a plastic
surgeons' convention. Forty to two
hundred dollars each, depending on
how many teeth are left unbroken.
He buys in India but will have to stop
in August, a new law. I tell him
no, that that was when I thought death
was cute, like Sarah Bernhardt, with her Hamlet
prop and sleeping every night in
a coffin. Before all those hours in
the hospital doing crosswords, afraid to read
a novel in case I ran across words like
"love," or "alone," or "wife." Before she
opened her eyes and said it looks like you're finally
going to be free. Or before I quit
smoking and started jogging because the man
in the next room, gross and wheezing, was swelling
every day, slowly exploding like something already
dead in the sun. Before I found out I was happy and
always have been.
Pretty soon, my friend says,
all skulls will be plastic, and we talk
about fishing again in the Gulf, how
we're going to stand waist deep in that jade
water, how we're going to bust those trout, really
put ants on them, how we're going to let them go.

Nothing's Been the Same Since John Wayne Died

My world isn't hers, skin
like mocha coffee she climbs
into each morning, air pouring
through her throat clear
as creek water, no line where
brown legs slide into
silk shorts. She's my student
but I'm in class now, aerobics,
flunking in a room of convex
mirrors and dumbbells, though
she's patient, pities me, the
sounds I make for air. It's
hopeless as a dancing bear, Disney
hippo in a tutu, a friend's
father. She wants to pop
candy in my mouth when I do
something right. To her, cigarettes
smell like burning celery, liquor
is shellac, her heart has a slow
beat and sticks to it, she can bench press
me. I sort of pity *her,* daughter
I never had, how far she has
to go, how dirty and heavy.
But she's perfect now, and even
her hard music gets under my
fat, sets my frog leg jumping
in jean stores.
She's working hard to get me young,
I'm aging her fast,
and three times a week
we keep meeting here.

Our Father Who Art On Third

> *After all he said to himself, it is probably only insomnia.*
> *Many must have it.*
> —"A Clean, Well-Lighted Place"

I stopped praying years ago, learned how
to think, instead, of love or the icy mountains before
death, green fields beyond. Now I need
a quiet god, not to make the heart rattle,
a golf ball in a cup. Baseball fits best,
almost as if designed in sleep: the pick-off, brush-
back, squeeze, suicide squeeze, stealing. It's no
heaven—it's here: slick skin and stitches of the ball
in hand reminding me of Ebba St. Claire, Atlanta
Cracker catcher built like crossed trees, showing us
how to throw, the ball an egg in the knotted
roots of his fingers. If he never made it, how
can we? Yet I wear before sleep the welts
and wrinkles of a glove, dream hand, grip the bone
handle of a Louisville Slugger, slap clay
from my spikes and go toward the dark as to
home, playing for the bunt, the sacrifice.

From
HOW THE DEAD BURY THE DEAD

University of Akron Press, 1994

How the Dead Bury the Dead

This should have been the question
to Jesus, not *why*, all that philosophy,
but *how*, a little scientific curiosity.
Maybe it became a disciple joke. The answer?
With a pick and shovel? They'd giggle to themselves as they
straggled behind him. Or maybe the beginning of the knock
knock joke, most Biblical humor being
morbid, Martha saying of poor
Lazarus, *But, my Lord, by now he stinketh,* and breaking
everyone up.

But nobody asked or wrote it down. What difference could it make
then, so near eternal life? But in those Dead Sea caves
was neither handbook nor *The Disciples' Big Book o' Jokes,*
which is a tragedy. Think about the savings!
Or the quiet, kissless wakes because
no one has lips. Or tears. Or casket wood to choose.
And what else have they got to do? Bone idle, the British
say. And that was the way he said it, *Let the dead bury
their own dead,* as if they'd been waiting to, the real unemployed.

Perhaps it's a potion you pour, a dust sprinkled on the
graves that pulls them to the top
like Clearasil. Maybe just leaving the bodies at
the edges of graveyards at sundown
or wrapped on the curbs like garbage bags
brings them like the tooth fairies they were as apprentices.
From our beds we'll hear the clacking and sliding of knuckles
on the handles like more bones, and in the morning they'll be gone
beneath another anthill, and we'll be about
our business, their lives vanishing behind us
like dreams. And aren't there more
important things to do? After all, where were they going
in such an all-fired hurry they couldn't even take
the time to stick somebody in the ground?

Oh. And the answer? Almost anywhere. And as quickly as possible.

Yards

He had no luck with yards.
I made sure my first
was flat, square, spongy, etched
with mower tracks, daffs
already sprouting. But the last owner
took his thumbs with him, and I fear
the curse, the lawn already
tilting into a hill that sluices
rain, turns Georgia-red, gullies,
bleeds. My father's bulbs popped up
and rolled away like turnips
through fire ant cones, over
fireweed and gristle of crabgrass runners.
No matter what he threw down, fescue,
St. Augustine, Kentucky Bluegrass,
we'd come home to find it draining
seeds and manure into the neighbor's
turf thick as peat. Why weren't
we happier? The mower slid sideways
down the hill, bogged its tricycle
tires, the blade spit rock
into his shins, spewed dust in his face.
I went back to one, the worst,
catty-cornered on the lot, and stared
at the perfect lawn, the hill he swore at, called
impossible, now flat as a green.
Even his grave is bare.

Hardheads

for Matt

Out in the brown tidal river, the snow of herons
and gulls covered mangrove islands. The sun rose
from dawn to full morning, the bridge hotter, whiter,
so still and quiet you could almost hear
the tide rising to cover holes of fiddler crabs
in black mud. Nothing but hardheads, with the slimy spine
that could puncture rubber soles, and one ray
whipping its tail, belly a white face
working, gills sad, down-turned clown eyes.

My grandfather, if it wasn't an Ex-Lax morning,
with his rusted reel and dry-rotted line;
my huge horny-handed plumber uncle
who'd untangle whiskery line all morning
out of the bottoms of his bifocals, smiling;
his son, blond brother to me; my father, fishing
for the aristocratic sea trout he never caught,
his captain's hat, his rod pulling the current
like a question mark. *There he is!* he'd shout
and whip his rod around, knocking off his hat.
That was a definite strike. Then back to waiting
as the sun moved toward afternoon.

All dead now. Plastic reels. A hook through shrimp
that wanted loose from shell. The plumb bob of sinker
to reach the bottom, catch another one,
my uncle laying down his rod, smiling, poking pliers
down the bony throat, throwing it back
to splash beneath the grid they raised
for the marlin-gaffed boats of fat men drinking beer,
headed for the blue. Sometimes a car would come by,
fanning us with hot air, tires bumping
on the tarry seams of the bridge
like heartbeats. And after, the silence
I haven't heard since.

Anniversaries

1.

It's hard to believe you've missed my wife
and your grandson, twenty-five years of fishing
and funny movies.
Every day you sleep
past breakfast, past supper.
What are you listening to
down in your room, your head
tilted toward the dark?
What dream is so beautiful it cannot spare you?

2.

Soon I'll be the age you are
forever, the day you pulled
off the interstate, your heart
boiling like a cracked block,
to die in a phone booth
while everyone passed you by.

We'll be twins—
I see us coming in the amber of store windows.
The next day I'll be
the eldest, you
tagging along to some
place you've already been.

Already you could be my mother's son.
Someday you could be mine.
Maybe then you'd listen
when I told you to stay
off the fatty foods and the interstates,
to slow down and stay well.
To grow old. To call.

Hands

for Phil Brady

When he died she felt
beneath the sheet for his hands,
which once were indigo, orange,
on her back in the jukebox glow,
now failed and beautiful
as Dührer's, cooling
to blue,
and then the nurse wept too.

She wanted to remember them,
the feel of them in her own,
the way they try to remember
themselves, hands, by carving bark,
hollowing clay,
memorizing on the cave wall,
tapping, fingering the stops
and the valves that follow the pen,
or painting with, plucking and weaving,
the hair of the dead.

They begin tracing
their shape on paper, pressing
signatures in sand.
They end scribbling
like crabs,
reading the braille
of faces,
trembling,
feeding quarters
to the wrong dream.

Tying A Tie

I saw you naked
only once, walking from the bedroom
to the bath. I'd never seen hair
that black. When you came back
you held a towel there.
Once I watched while you put on
one of those starched white shirts,
tucking the tails between your legs.

But I needed to know the right
way to shower, wash my hair, shave.
Or how to tie a tie,
a Windsor knot or that other one.
Maybe you didn't know.
I still don't know
if I do things right,
if everybody reaches through their fly
and pulls their underpants down to pee.

Much less sex. So when I got
into trouble, you said, *You've
destroyed everything we ever tried to build
up in this community.*
And God forbid I ever miss church four times
a week, even once a year to watch
The Wizard of Oz on Sunday night.
I still dream about those nos,
wake up crying, pounding on your chest
even in your coffin. You don't seem to
mind, or even notice.
God comes first, you said.

Well, God has you now, maybe teaching you
about that loop on the back
of the big end that the little end goes through.

First Love

When they found out we wanted to get married
they stopped us from seeing each other,
and we had to sneak around until
I left for college. I finally cut
my wrists and sent a dozen roses,
writing *goodbye* on the card with my
bandaged hand. She went and married
somebody else. That family was too
close anyway, calling I love you
through the walls at night.
I didn't know about Freud then.

The last time Mother saw her she had
two kids and weighed in around two
hundred, which is two hundred too few.
I wonder if her husband rides
a motorcycle like her father did.
He wouldn't understand poetry,
how you can't hit a pothole with it,
or slide a hundred yards on gravel,
showing the scars of leather
to your son-in-law. He's probably
dead by now, and I liked him.

After twenty years, this started out as my
revenge, but turned into a typical
poem: a motorcycle, two kids, some
scars, and a fat wife calling
I love you through the walls at night.

Small Road to Nowhere

I live on a hill with troubles,
mine, every one of them, everywhere
like the struck-back teeth of cemeteries.
The last one I had to haul up
myself, and it almost killed me.
But now it sits quiet in the back room,
dusty, tied like a ham and still
as the swing in the front yard
where gnats swarm and orbit an atom.
I only go to town for feed
and seed and haircuts where the pole
spools its red, white, and blue ribbons
endlessly. Two chairs, no waiting.

Skin

Something's under it like moles,
prickling like cold wind rippling a lake,
sucking like a magnet thrums the telephone's
membrane burring out its bad news.
Skin is your friend:
imagine a big frog leg, flayed,
wind and sand on bare muscles, rain
in grooves sluicing bones, and you
know why slick organ bags glue
skin like wet paper.

It's the first to go—in earth,
peppering like buckshot, in fire,
shrinking and crackling.
Because it never bleeds it's
the part lovers love, smooth to the
tongue and sweet smelling,
covering stuff like chicken gizzards
in blond gristle, the package we don't
want to open. Its mouths like
curtains open to let us in so far,
where a backdrop hides the gears and pulleys.
It's not the actor we want anyway,
but the character, in pancake and greasepaint.
It's the story we want, the shallow,
happy ending, not the asides, the
parenthesis that says beauty's
only skin deep, because that's
deep enough.

Bayou

I don't go to the Gulf anymore
to wade out before dawn from shore
into water warmer than the air,
gulls and dolphins everywhere,
and, feeling with my feet the washboard sand,
shuffle to the edge of where I stand
and, having gone as far as I can go,
cast my line toward Mexico.

I live now where color gives in to snow,
but I feel in my blood how they know
in the fall to enter the marshes, out
of the roughening sea, the trout
moving in on an autumn tide
to feed on the shrimp and crabs that hide
in the prairie edge of green sawgrass,
the sky finally blue with the first pass
of northern air so strong
reeds bend that were straight all summer long.

These tidal rivers become in dreams
skewed kinds of Northern streams—
theater or supermarket aisle,
a furniture showroom with pile
carpet rippled like sand
under water now clear, where I stand
on sofa, or island of cans, and cast
to where I saw their fin-flick last.
And when nothing I own will make them bite,
I jump from bed to bed in fluorescent light,
from room to room, following behind
their search for the sea they'll never find.

And finally, near dawn, snow falling outside,
the fish begin moving in my own tide,
ebbing in the dark aisles of me,

looking for an inland sea
where tides and weather
are quiet together,
and the dark water in the smallest bay
rises and falls on the heron's leg
barely an inch all day.

Rust Belt

After a year here we learn
they have a name, *Beaters*—
the ones without insurance
who don't give a shit,
who drive out-of-control
toboggans and just hope they slide
into one of those Jap cars with their huge
rusted Chevies, Fords, Pontiacs
with the big names, eaten so bad
they're just frames.
He gets welfare for cigarettes
and lotto, limps through the grocery
buying dented cans and no-name stuff,
leaves mufflers and tail pipes
in the road, curses me in my car
he didn't make, didn't pour
into a mold then piece together
because some hotshot thought small
cars were a fad, no fins.
He snorts at the poetry reading
in the paper, *Poems. That's all*
we're makin' now,
and after the reading, while
we're out looking at the Amish drive
their black sleighs, he keys a Subaru, slips
skating across the parking lot in old shoes,
and cheap wine drips from the bag
like a lung. If we were there we couldn't help
laughing, and he wouldn't even mind
because he knows people like us,
the ones who think they'll somehow get to the future
before he does.

The Original Adam and Eve

They've been found in Mesopotamia,
Ohio, in a sideshow, "unearthed"
says the canvas where he's painted
a pink David, she, Botticelli's Venus,
a python coiled between like a stack
of tires, tongue forking the air.
Inside they're enough
to demand your money back,
"serpent" segmented and thin
as a worm, bat's pointed ears and pig
nose, still tangled in her legs
like the cord of a child who is gone.
She's four feet tall, so hairy,
her small breasts almost invisible,
grasping feet cupping air, sad
monkey face.
He's maybe an inch taller, fingers
crabbed with arthritis,
side squashed in where the rib was.
The fig leaves are faded gray as bay leaves
and brittle, broken to show their sex
shrunken, almost gone.
The government has stepped in,
and after a long tour they'll be buried
for good, two little hills with a ridge between.

Tool

It's never the right one, size
or place, like love, whose names,
just as violent as vice—vise
grip, screw, straight-slot screwdriver,
wrench, socket—try to hold
together what doesn't want
to fit. Violent as my preacher father
building the cross that would be
my racer, no drill (how
often would he use one, anyway?), just
swearing and hacking that
bolt hole into an axle not even
Samson could turn with just a
rope. Half my fiber was splinters of
telephone poles. But he did one thing
right, at least once, because everything's
a tool when you need it, and the best are
near to hand, adjustable,
like the vise of chin and chest
when you dress a pillow
or that jack handle that can raise a woman
and you with her.

Advent

Kids have sprayed the boulder
orange, given it
black eyes, a stitched
mouth. My neighbor tells
about the ferry, how birds
at the edge of Erie, whirling
in the white skies like pepper,
wait for blue weather, play
statues with a winter
that can open one gray eye
and freeze them halfway
across. We hang suet,
sow millet, as if winter
were another crop, snow warm
as cotton, sleet nourishing
as rice we would die without.
The leggy marigolds we pulled up
lie on the driveway
still pushing out their suns,
and we begin piling leaves,
stuffing them in plastic
sacks, stacking
the pillows so high
it must seem to the circling
birds, to the squirrels in their
holes, to the knuckleheaded
jack-o'-lantern in the park,
that we are hoping someone
will fall and save us.

Tenderhooks

a found poem

My students live in houses
on the second floor, are just passengers
on the card game of life,
and are sometimes left dangling in left field.
They've had their brains washed out
and don't see the umpire's new clothes.

And this innocence complicates even
their young love, is why they put
their women on pedastools,
don't see why we shouldn't mount
the rear end of a dear as well as the front,
see the partner's misery in the other half
of a felationship, see towers and trees
as phalanx symbols, need two to tangle,
forget to include diaphragms
in their research papers, and thus
take love for granite.

But they also know, from the standpoint
of observation, that we have become so content
on making snap judgments
that we often make them in haste,
that sex is becoming more freely practiced
by the general public to satisfy
their sexual needs and desires,
and that almost half of all pregnancies
occur within six months of intercourse.
That William B. Yeast gave rise
to modern poetry. That Chaucer took the nut
of love, cracked it, and laid the meat on the table.
That it is necessary that society abandon
its prejudices, and behave respectably
under the pretense that homosexuals
are human beings.

They use their brains and not just their bronze.
They do not go Gentile into that good night.
And if they have to shoot, they only shoot
the fat. They know
the cloud with the silver lining
will pull through. They are a Godscent.

All of Us Are Children

floating down a river on our beds.
It's dark, and we're in pajamas,
though in the west, behind
the palms, there's a thread
of pink, a glow of violet,
as if we've just come in from play.
Each bed has a paper lantern
and we see each other in the glow.
Parents watch from verandas on the shore,
drinking together and hushing us,
but it does no good. When we're almost
quiet, giggling starts again
and spreads like wind over water.
Our beds are so close they nudge,
tip, and lap,
and goldfish rise to the light
through the reflections
of our faces.
Then the river opens
into a sea
we begin to fill
like a whole new sky,
and we are the stars.

Seventh Heaven

The first is just long, years and years to see how "more time" was just an excuse. You still don't learn to play the violin. You blame your parents.

This takes a while, a lot of umbrage taking, yelling, like a long Thanksgiving dinner. You blame yours, they blame theirs, you all cry, apologize, that sort of thing.

The third is sex, getting it out of the way, fifty years tops to work through combinations, permutations. By the end, you're sick of skin, and irritable. If only you'd gotten the chance the first time.

Bosses, cheerleader and Nobel committees, coaches and pro scouts, all the way back to Miss Marcus in the second grade, now they're impressed. You were the greatest thing since angel food. They apologize.

You need a rest. For the first two thousand, you do, you rest, but you hit the wall at four, think you're going to crack, so much solitude. It's as if you're a mountaintop, snow and clouds, all glare and wind. But you don't crack, or if you do it's more the snapping of a flag.

It's just more loneliness at first, six is, sort of like those first days of all your deaths, disoriented, cold. You're squeaking like something in the wind, splashing like a shore.

There are thoughts, feelings, and memories but they're loosening leaves. There's the smell of smoke and lots of sky. You almost feel like letting go, falling.

You do.

The History of Effects

The Bible was created by Bishop Ussher
in 4004 B.C. Then Galileo cooked the universe
too long, and the earth, like a yolk, slipped off
center and everything began to wobble.
Freud needed a reason to talk about sex,
and Marx wrote a bestseller
so he could retire rich.
When the species started to hunt
for their origin, they discovered Darwin.

So now the ears of corn put down
tethers to the earth, trees rake
the wind into piles, the sun turns the world
like a ballerina, like a magnet whirls
a rotor. Silence squelches the radios,
and darkness the bulbs. Automobiles are invented
to reach the malls, and choppers to haul
body bags, and animals come to live with us
to quench our loneliness and nourish our hunger.
We've begun to love the people who need us
as dandruff rises from sweaters to infect our hair,
and parachutes are the white flags
of suicides that fail.

Hypochondria

This week it's bladder
cancer for her, for me
Lou Gehrig's. You feel it
first in the wrists, like ice
water. But as Delmore Schwartz,
a famous sick man, once said,
even paranoids have enemies
and sometimes a cigar is just
exploding.
And someday it will come
for us, in some clothes or
other, some face, running
over the poppy fields like a perfume commercial.
Then we'll say we told you
so, and you'll feel a twinge
of guilt, and then another
in the back and just below
the shoulder blade, near the what,
the spleen?

Entrance

It's one of those days you wait for
all summer as if all your life.
Cool air has come blowing all day,
flickering tired green leaves.
You're so happy you could cry,
and do, don't even care
if the drugstore's out of pills
because your brother's found work,
a building crew, wood butchers who
could use some part-time help,
like his smile, and care less
if he never drives a nail.
So to the park, where,
remember, wind is springwater, quenching
the skin, blowing like a fall
you walk around in with the one
you loved most,
though everybody ever is there,
walking your way.
And the question is,
do you love them all, equally?

Sorry. Begin again.

It's one of those days you wait for
all summer as if all your life.

From
SIMMER DIM

University of Akron Press, 1999

The Silkie

We know what those old songs
and stories are really about—
bairns born wet and cauled
to Shetland maidens visited
by the nameless in the night—
thick black whiskers, slick side
and bullet shape in the green sea
of dream, lingering smell of low tide
in the room, brine in the fur.
And then she marries the harpooner,
a good steady man,
and gets old,
as stories have her held
in swan-foot flippers, down
the seal-king's women taken,
their weed-hair water-waves
on roof the awful house of his,
forever with him dwell in thrall,
memory the surge-light
that pierces gloom of deep sea-hall.

Footpaths

> *Jon Anderson, my Jo Jon*
> *We've climbed the hill together,*
> *And many a canty day, Jon,*
> *We've had with one another.*
> —Robert Burns

This is why we came, these tracks
through farmyard and field,
around rusted harrows as the farmers work,
their border collies crazy-eyed at us
as two more things to organize, direct,
although our feet already trace
the steps of sheep and cows, between
the green pools of slurry, here
where no fence, nothing private,
can stop us legally
because the dead,
lying in the churchyards of these valleys,
have stamped a seal into this clay
and put a stile over every obstacle.

Even in dreams, I follow
a stenciled yellow arrow on the walls
of train stations, into toilets,
over stiles, through a window
into an alley, nowhere I can't go,
until the trees thicken
and I can't fit between, or through
contractions of a farmhouse window,
my body outside, my head left stuck
on the sill, cooling like a pie.

We've walked hundreds of miles like this;
our maps weary at the fold,
we point like dueling compasses,
our shadows hesitating
on the sundial of a field,

our feet always after another
dotted line or hedged-in lane.
We know how long a wrong turn takes,
have come to hate the forks,
and tire of saying *the road not taken.*

We travel well, you say;
it's home where we get lost.
On the tops of hills as our breathing slows
we've learned the price of every view,
measure our desire against the ever
steeper climb and even steeper fall,
where the knees almost want to fail,
give in, to just let go and run,
as if we'd be able to stop.

The colors this November
still have a way to go,
and though the summer was warmer
than ever before, the winter
has taken no offense so far.
Has a winter ever never happened?
They say there's a valley near
no frost has ever touched,
and though we have no map,
why should that stop us now?
As long as we can see at least the ghosts
of other steps across the field,
let's take this path through woods,
and the long climb over the hill.

Blodeuwedd

There's a folktale here of a lonely man
who married a woman, wizard-woven,
her name Blodeuedd, Welsh for flowers.
He held her in his arms like a long
bouquet, like the leggy roses
of beauty queens.

Like the one I cut my wrists for,
who danced with another boy.
Like the one here in this other land
thirty years along,
though I'm too tired and old
to bleed again.

You know what comes next,
roses prone to withering, to
falling petal by petal from
their stems—she was fragile
and fell in love with someone else.

So his wizard father, angry,
tweaked her name a letter more
and from flowers she was made
a flower-face, the owl,
doomed to fly with chrysanthemum eyes
alone at night and shunned
by other birds.

End of story. As Arthur lost
to Lancelot, with good grace, Guinevere,
who ended alone in a nunnery,
the hills and woods outside her cell
blurred with fog like a bridal veil.

Now he must lie by the side
of a new, white bride and hear
the small rain whisper on the windowpanes,

listen through the bare-leaved
twined-with-ivy trunks
and branches of the winter woods
for the sound a punished woman makes,
her wings flailing at the dark air
like twining fingers in her lover's hair,
crying, not *who, who, who,*
but still, even now, *where, where?*

At Arthur's Stone

They say on simmer dim this stone will stand
then walk the long slope down to Burry to drink.
At the winter solstice, hand-in-hand

for now, the truce between us holding for a while,
we walk the frosted rusty red
of autumn fern, past a moldering pile

of wild Welsh pony bones,
to see the grave of an early king,
a stone balanced long ago on other stones.

We touch its blotched gray flank
as millions have, for luck,
as though solidity and poise, its blank

face could cure us of our yearnings, keep
our lives together till we die.
Nearby's a cairn of those like us, a heap

of stones too numerous to name, too small
to walk, that marks the grave of men
who dragged or sailed it here to rest on tall

and humpbacked Cefn Bryn, to overlook the bay
of cockle sands that glisten when the tide is out,
and be the shrine of girls who came to lay

milk-soaked honey cake upon the ground
before this altar stone,
and crawl three times around,

and if her love were true he would appear,
transported from whatever distant place,
easing through the mist to meet her here.

The moon comes up behind a pony white
as a unicorn; the sun goes down
and pinks the sky and bay before the night

recalls this postcard from the past.
Too far away to see the cars
and houses with their shipwreck masts

of washing poles and satellite dishes,
we might be a pelted pair of ancient,
shivering, short-lived, walking wishes

staring at the mound where we will lie.
And every longest day, the sun
will squint between the lids of sea and sky

that never close, and from this height—
as we dream our centuries of thirst
through the long, pink, dying light—

like a mote in an eye that cannot blink,
the stone of one who lost his love
will walk to the sea to drink.

Welsh Courier Braves Daylight

The book we ordered didn't come in.
It didn't get put
on the van, she says.
Maybe next week.

Things are different here.
We order our turkey
from Rees the Meat
who hands it to us
in a flurry of feathers,
though he doesn't know why,
what Thanksgiving is.
The little watchmaker,
in his element
of Dickensian ticking,
declines to tackle
my electric watch.
The fishmonger says,
I don't know.
Crabs is crabs.
The kind with little legs.

Out on the blue bay
draining to low tide,
fishing boats bob
to find bottom;
wild ponies have picked the gate
to eat our garden,
and sheep wander the roads
like blown batting.
Our e-mail won't work,
and the fax and photocopy
are in the village
in the model train store.
I watch the tiny cars
trace rails through matchbox coal towns,
through pipe-cleaner trees.

We're living here this year
five time zones away
from all we thought,
and if we miss something
we've learned to let it go,
to have another pint,
knowing whatever it is
just might come on the van
next week,
or around the cape if the seas are mild,
on muleback
if the snows don't clog the pass.

Hooks

In the Gulf, where my wife almost died
one day, crabbing in the hot sun,
and where that Kate Chopin heroine waded out
to drown herself, I caught a banana fish,
the Daffy Duck of the sea. When I made
the rookie mistake of keeping the rod bent,
the fish dithered and threw the hook into my thumb.
I remembered movies about Indians and arrows,
and tried to push it through, to cut off
the barb, but the edges of my sight grew black,
like a crepe-hung portrait of a thumb.

Along the bayou, across the salt march,
my wife drove as I lay in the back seat, where
she would lie two years later, vessels
about to burst in her brain.
As we drove over bridges of happy fishermen
who didn't even know they were happy,
I thought of mountain men dragging bear-broken legs
miles to trading posts, and felt weak and silly,
and then, when we got to the hospital in Golden Meadow,
humiliated when the Cajun nurse said, *You muss not be
from around heah,* and I looked at the big board under glass,
all of the hooks and lures pulled out,
and from what parts of the tourist body told,
and they were all there—earlobes,
balls, eyelids, eyeballs. Once, long
after all this, I clipped from the newspaper
the story of a man standing behind his wife
when she cast. *It hurt so bad,* he said,
I couldn't even yell, so his wife pulled back
and gave another yank. It took hours
of surgery to dig two prongs of that treble hook
out of his nostrils.

My wife didn't die, I'm happy
to report, and I became a better person,
I think. So that's why, after the doctor
gave me my shot and pulled with a sound
like a leaf tearing, what he held up
I see now as a kind of symbol, like a bullet
wearing a hula skirt.

Bread of Heaven

As I walked out under this first spring
day, tower bells tolled an old hymn,
in my memory a heaven of Welsh miners,
their mouths open like baby birds.
They remind me how far I've come from chapel,
how what I worship now is more
the mouths themselves, so hungry for something
from a great mute god throned elsewhere.
It's hunger now that's sweet for me,
voices surpassing what they sing to
or for, the only god our great
emptiness the wind makes music of.
Mozart and Shakespeare are, finally,
their pain, out of chapel, swaying all night
on the moor, on the frozen thorn.
The birds build nests again this year
for babies that are born to freeze or fly,
either way their hearts agape,
while I worship not a god of light
but yearning itself, that has many
sweet voices, sweetest as they die,
and pray to the dark god that made
the world and lets it cry.

The Last Holiday

Spetses, Greece 1996

Here on the pebbled beach by the wine-dark sea,
we ache for what we know—the white sand and aqua
of the Gulf of Mexico—though light here silvers
the leaf tips of the olive trees, grass between
as golden as the autumn vines of Tuscany,
and houses bleached like skulls
on the Day of the Dead in Mérida,
cicadas grinding like all the pepper mills
of high season in Provence.
The clothesline flaps its flag of one white shirt:
The Espresso Bean, Cannon Beach, as if to say
my body went to Oregon, but all I got was memory.
Now, this place too will be the ever youthful
body of another lover we have lost.

How many summers have we left?
Our suntans wrinkle like packed clothes,
our hair grows a sea-salt grizzle,
sunsets bleed in the whites of our eyes.
Perhaps it's not too late to seek another shore,
with pines like these in Cézanne chunks of green,
strung like the sponges of Tarpon Springs,
the water warm as rum, gin-and-tonic
fizzy and clear, where we plan to go
next year, if we're still alive,
and where, no doubt, we'll pine for Greece
with all of yearning's yin and yang,
as oceans spin their spiral galaxies of shells,
and down in the garden lemons
hang like a thousand suns.

From
ASCENDING ORDER

University of Akron Press, 2003

Them

How many of those '50s movies were about people
who weren't people, whose bodies had been snatched.
But the small-town someplace was always
Hollywood, the sepia night filtered day,
the spaceships plywood, the instruments just
more televisions and Christmas lights,
the monsters rubber
or daubs of paint on celluloid.
We must have been afraid
of who we were in our split levels,
Father remote behind his newspaper,
driving the finned car to rendezvous in caves
with more of his kind, networked by telepathy,
Mother in high heels, carrying the alien seed,
looking for dust, like the heroine who
screamed so well, her rayoned breasts
ack-ack guns propped at the sky in vigilance.
They'd never let her leave town, roadblocks
everywhere, and called her crazy when she told
how her husband wasn't the man she married,
how the kid upstairs in his room
was planning to take over,
be one of them.

A Woman Brought to Child

The second law is that the bad news is always
worse than the good news is good:
I won a prize,
and my only sister died.

She never had a chance.
I remember cowering while
our parents upstairs screamed
at each other again about her grades, until
she stood up, threw down her schoolbooks,
and began screaming, too.
If anything happened, it happened
to her: nickname Stinky, coonskin cap
with the plastic pate stamped *Davvy
Crockett,* tonsils, appendix, wren
bones breaking, green eyes behind
batwing glasses, the boys
staying away. Algebra
chased her from nursing school
like nausea, then a brick Bible
college, a redneck marriage, and losing
her babies to the county.

Barmaid, she was trying
to start again when I left her
drunk on the doorstep that
Christmas ten years ago, gave me that old
picture of her as Shirley Temple with
a cowboy hat, white taps, red
sequined cuffs that swayed to "Pony Girl."
Her new man stayed inside with his
cartoons and vodka in that month's
dump, as she said goodbye
for the last time, hugged her new
daughter, wept, and waved.

You know the story—it's the one
the private eye tells about finding
the guilty, who done in the floating
body of the woman with no last name,
the first something rich, like Candy
or Ginger, who somehow got lost
and fell in with bad companions.
Somewhere near the end of the movie,
the gumshoe finally tracks the family
down and shows them the picture
of the woman they hardly recognize, yellow
and withered, and they show him the picture
of the little girl they remember—
squinting into the sun, standing
in the doorway to the rest of her life, waving
goodbye, her jelly bread falling
jelly side down.

Cupidity

We all called him Butt Breath,
something inside him tainted,
why he walked home—shambling,
pigeon-toed—from the bus stop alone.
Why I shot him with an arrow
through the cheek, so grateful
I'd play with him, he didn't tell
my mother.
And then he found
her, black and white,
hidden in his father's darkroom:
young, beautiful, hair
so black and thick we couldn't
see through it there
between her open legs.
We fought over her, folded her
so small to fit her hiding places
that the paper creased white, as if
she were in jail.
The final fight ripped her,
and he got the bottom. I
still have her small breasts
and face, happy to show us
all she had, her smile an arrow
in both of us forever.

The Poet, Calling the Kettle Black

I name to myself my students
as if we were all Indians—
to my left the beautiful
Two Kids in Play School,
in front, the shaggy
Car Won't Start,
to my right the timid
Cries over Commas.
Perhaps because a student says
I was her Hopi father
in another life,
this comes naturally to me, and I
expect to overhear in the men's room
complaints about old Dry as Dust,
or Where Was I, or
Sleep Bringer.

My sister was, and still is,
Jelly Side Down,
my brother, No Forwarding Address,
and where would I be without my love,
It's My Fault?

I can almost remember being rocked
to sleep each night after I had climbed
into my cliff house,
my mother, Cry More and You'll Pee Less,
fighting with her husband, Will
of God, then crooning lullabies
to the infant If He'd Set Out to Fail
He Could Not Have Done Worse,
or baby Zircon in The Rough,
little Bluffing with Diddly.

Priscilla

for Patty

My student, who has been *regressed*
many times, through all her other lives,
says she knew me on a ship, and we
were married, though not to each other.
The ship went down, and I, a woman,
got put on a lifeboat with my children.
She, a man, drowned saving the children
of others. She says my child is now
her nephew, shows me his photo
to see if I recognize him (her?). I don't,
but tell her this means nothing since
I'm the least transmigratory
of any soul I know—although
it's only noon, I'm thinking of
a heaven of martinis after a day
of work.

Being a woman, I never got
the insurance money I was owed.
Maybe that's why
you've got poetry now, she says.
I don't disbelieve any of this.
In fact, tonight I'll try to have a drink
with her, try hard to remember her face
in a sea-salt tarnished mirror,
or the faces of children. Perhaps
I'll begin to dream of her, a breakthrough—
she'll wander through my house at night,
wondering over TVs and tapping keyboards,
while I marvel at the pewter ruffles
of the silk dress where a small, wet head
wept between my breasts.

First Impression

I don't look like anyone, but
a woman I met the other day
called me Liam Neeson, though
she said it Lie Am, my star's face
slightly askew like the slew of a stick
thrust through the torque of water,
the Roman nose of a boxer pushed aside
by a Picasso punch. We all
have a double somewhere, they say,
maybe the other side of someone else's
wonderful life, a poor man's Jimmy Stewart
who takes the rap for embezzlement and falls
just short of what is wanted, another
beautiful face, but squinted through
the smudge of a thumbprint glass,
faded like a photo taken from
the amniotic developer too soon.
Even Adam with his matinee curls,
reclining on the rolled and pleated couch
of clay on the Sistine ceiling, is not
being touched by the finger of God, but,
by a trick of perspective, pointed
past, to what He really meant: not you,
Adam, with your orangutan arms and tree-thick
trunk, but him, him back there, the willowy
pretty boy right behind you.

Prostrate

When the barber sees my hair, his eyes
widen, his ancient clippers pause in the air,
humming like flies' wings. I bring her father,
hobbling with a cane, among these old
Mississippi farmers wearing overalls
and white socks, to trim his gray fringe.
It's like a general store, and they talk
of guns and deer, crops and weather,
their joints and scars and the sawing
through breastbones, while I look at *People*
and the walls of rifles and plows,
the hung, gray, papery wasps' nests
swollen big as pumpkins around their limbs,
Vitalis, axes, whip saws and band saws,
and lots of antlers, the splay
of rattlers' skins. I think
of the rubber catheter squirming loose
and slippery as a tentacle, the blood
on his underwear and sheets, my dreams
of erections, liver-spotted.
Two artillery shells stand waist-high
in the corner. The barber says,
like a TV evangelist or Bible prophet,
I don't care what you do, if you're
*man of woman born you will **not** get out*
of this life without prostrate.
After a mere twelve minutes and the four
dollars it's always been, I lead her father
away like the blind Samson, the others
watching, the only sound now the buzzing
that makes their short hair shorter.

Breedlove

Where were you, my Breedlove,
my elegant guitar, when I was choked
and cramped with puberty, stiff, clumsy
fingers bleeding from hours of fondling
my Sears and Roebuck "Les Paul"?
I learned the chords before I could even tune
the thing and twanged "John Henry" and "Blowin'
in the Wind" in Japanese. Nor did
I fare better with the delicate
instrument Arleen McKee.
What I needed was a grown woman
to show me the pearl inlays, struts
and grooves, the smoothly turning keys
and lightly fingered frets of harmony.

So I apologize to Arleen, whose fault
it wasn't, though her shape, too,
symbolized my mistuned youth: big
and blonde with fertility goddess
hips and a chest well-rounded
as Monroe's or Mansfield's
and a soundhole I could never
free the music from.

Waiting in the Flu Line

The first ten yards aren't bad, tall
plastic columns of colored candy
on one side of the aisle, humorous
greeting cards on the other that we reach
for and read, chuckling, shaking our heads,
shuffling through fluorescence. It's
"At Risk" day, and though I'm diabetic,
the others look suspiciously at my relative
youth and low body fat. But that
winter my wife lay in our tiny bed
and I on the floor in another room, both
too weak to even cook a can of soup,
until finally a friend brought food
and ice cream, the melting scoops little
clown faces with M&M noses
and dunce cap cones.

Now I'm up to the serious cards,
condolences for death and disease,
and there's nowhere to look but
up ahead to more candy wall or the gum-wad
hearing aid in the ear in front, until
we reach the religious cards of crosses, lilies,
and angels. Everyone seems to know
everyone else, the couples hold
hands, and I wonder if it will feel
this way in the long line down
to the landing where we board
the boat, if I will be alone
there, too, my useless arms finally
needed for a child, which I will have
to hand to the ferryman while I
stoop to drink, inoculation
against what I might carry
across, memories so beautiful
they are impossible to bear.

Aesop at Sixty

Sheepish, pleading a pulled
muscle, I limp like Hephaestus
past flocks of women in white
to whisper a question. My age,
Hippocrates wipes a whisker, smiles
and gives me samples on the sly.
I stutter, *It's not that I can't...it's just
a question of stamina* (the sleepy
hare, the plodding tortoise). He nods.
And then, there's the mind and its mouse-
gnaw of doubt, mere cunning no
longer enough to tempt the cock
from the tree.

The insurance will pay for nine
pills a month, he says. *Out of what
hat did they pull **that** number?* we wonder,
and I leave with nine chances in my pocket
to be sixteen again and sense already
the snapping of that last strand
imprisoning the lion pride that once
defied my parents, time, and tide,
that feeling six inches from the tape
and the prize of Aphrodite, three-balled
with a stiff wind and Atalanta
at my back, and the certainty
that not even Zeus himself
can stop me now.

Toad's Wild Ride

And as you are American, I would like you to pay
special attention to the turn signal indicator.
                    —English rental car agent, 1978

A motorcar, a motorcar, wheezed Toad,
sitting unhorsed and dazed in the dust,
then bought his own snorting, sneezing
thing. First time in England, fifty
thousand miles ago, they handed us keys,
showed us everything backwards,
then walked away. *What in God's name!*
I yelled at my first roundabout, a whirlpool
of tiny traffic instead of a stoplight (we trust
inertia; they trust momentum). But,
by the end of the trip, I felt like donning
duster, goggles, scarf; could brush and burnish
oncoming cars with my whoosh of onionskin air.
Cheerio, we'd cry as we careened around a turn, as if
headed for Ratty's house in Quarry Wood.

For twenty years, we've taken one-track
roads, dotted on the map like pinholes
in pie crust, backing up for tractors,
even for horses and dog walkers, though
it's not for tourist cars these banked and tunneled
turns were made, but sports cars curved
and swooping like Spitfires, exhaust
thudding off stone walls and hedgerows, swallows
and swifts weaving the wind just ahead of the bonnet,
dolphin surfing the prow-push of bug-flushing, flower-scented air.

Though we're no sports, we've goosed our share
of farmyard geese, scattered village swans and swains,
neighed the horses and boomed through woods
past country things, the sidelong flash

of fox, skirr of pheasant. And when we get
frog-fat and old, we'll take tour buses,
lumber the lanes, frighten cars of
young couples to vanish in reverse,
and look down on all we used to make
fly up like the driven dust we are.

Running the Body

Until I had to balance the blood,
weigh and inject what would burn
every crumb I put into it, I never
appreciated the body. How
would it be to run
it all? Every second, squirt
of tear or saliva here, goose
of bile there while pumping
the bellows lungs, palpating
organs, remembering juices
to sluice the stomach, and always
the bowels to be squeezed along,
kidneys wrung like a sponge.
The mind's a flashing
switchboard always swamped
with what has just been sighted,
smelled, heard, sounds on the track
that projects on the old sheet
hanging back there in the dark.
And you, only two-handed when all
the lines start shrilling with fear
as the loved one draws near—
so many skills to learn! To sift
the sea-grass cilia of the nose,
to comb the coral
of the tongue, fill
the hollows with blood,
and, behind it all, an art:
the incessant and inconstant
timing of the heart.

From
FISHING AT THE END OF THE WORLD

Word Press, 2005

It's My Karma, and I'll Cry If I Want To

How do people survive who
listen to those oldies stations,
the psychic whiplash of your life,
the sad, happy, sad, happy bandstand mix
of your very own album, *Greatest Hits*
and Misses, any year ready to pounce
and only the DJ with his dance card
knows where you're going next?
As if a god, like Dick Clark after death,
showed you all your other lives—"(Sittin'
On) The Dock of the Bay," "There Goes
My Baby" with someone new, "Down
in the Boondocks"— and now you know why
you're in the song you are, that because
you fought the law and the law won,
you're working on a "Chain Gang"
and feel a "Bad Moon Rising."
And so we have to drink the waters of
forgetfulness, ferry cross the Mersey,
change channels, to live without memory, so
painful, so blue on blue, heartache
on heartache, that we won't recall
we knew each other before, smiled
at each other in the same way then,
but it turned out wrong—the screaming tires,
the busting glass—or right: Hey,
hey, Paula, I want to marry you.
Hey, Paul, I want to marry you, too.

Silly Mid-Off

It's the position
closest to the wicket, right
in front of the batsman,
unprotected, unhelmeted, as if
(I translate) the shortstop were
to stand barehanded between
the pitcher and the batter, except
a cricket ball is hard as wood.

I understand—he's there to head
off trouble, wants to stop it at
the source, the food
taster, scout into no-man's land,
see what's bad at first.
It's the suspense he hates worst,
that makes him willing to assume
this early place,
take it in the face so long
as there's no waiting to hear
about the love affair, the lab test,
that long drawn-out speech about
how it's all for the best.

It's why I keep watching John Wayne
in *The Alamo* and rereading
about the Donner party, fascinated
by the suicidal or cannibalistic,
the sexy combination of courage
and stupidity, like Napoleon
invading Russia, the speed of the Titanic
through the icebergs. Sophocles
had it wrong, Shakespeare right—
it's the flaws that draw us—who
cares about lightning bolts

from the blue, the skate
on the stair? We want the nude
midnight bath in the crocodile pool,
chain smoking, the drunken
car crash. We long to wrest
our deaths from the callous
hands of the cosmos and into
our own: tender, messy,
and mastering.

Waiting Rooms

We could write a guide to these
hotels of illness, our stars,
stitches or aspirins.
We're camp followers,
or families outside prisons
where the loved are being punished
and waiting for doctors
to look inside and tell them why.
My own princess is deep
in the maze, and though I can find her,
no kiss or song of mine can wake her,
nothing I can say or do
cut the bubbling tubes
unless he lets her go,
decides he will not keep her
yet.

In these rooms we light the first
True of our lives, watch *Let's
Make a Deal,* know the best nurses and
vending machines, each other's histories,
ask each morning did he have
a good night, are they letting you
go home today?

Always downstairs, we eat with the staff
the same food as the sick, nearer
to the clouds. Another machine foams diet
soda into cups like a brown river froth,
there's a salad bar because healthy
is happy, and they're happy to be
beneath the groans, urine, feces, blood
for a while, eating and drinking as if this
were already a wake, laughing as if a marriage
were going on upstairs—and why
not, with flowers everywhere
and everyone in white.

Mary Faye

Because you never admitted any
weakness, tonight there's a new gold
screw bolted in your hip, and I'm here
dreaming you're making me walk,
while you drive the car,
home in the rain
the way you made me walk to the football
you wanted me to practice.
Remember turning red, saying
Well I'll be when the doctor
showed you my shoulder on his
skeleton, fractured three days while
I cried in secret? Though you caught me
once and, as your father told you,
told me, laughing, *It'll put
hair on your chest.*

Now, again, as you close the door
of your red Corvette, the glass
swirls over your moving lips saying
without sound *It's a great life
if you don't weaken*
as you drive away.
Soon I'm far from any light,
soaked in cold water and lost in blowing
fog like the Scottish highlands.
But this isn't the nightmare.
The nightmare is this: because you may
be watching, I'm walking the best I can.

Finally

I was in Scotland buying tackle
when in came, of all people, you.
As I tried to explain,
somebody outside hooked
the big one; through
the window, yards of slick
skin and fluke. Everyone
ran out but me who stayed
to whisper could I come back.
You bowed your head and cried and said
no, that you'd only just healed.
I said no, not to hurt you
again. When you nodded, we
ran outside, just as they
hauled it out, and everybody
sat on it, and somebody took a picture.

Fishing at the End of the World

All currents converge at this island's
tip, in riffs and riptides, black
wave meeting black wave making
undertow, scooping the sand
floor so we can barely stand.
But, once a year, the bait
fish come in—pompano, a million
silver dollars ruffling the sea,
explode from the surf in sprays
when trout attack. Gulls shrieking
and falling, dolphins leaping and
twisting in sun, trout flashing
white around our knees, fifty
of us cast all directions at once, nylon
lines hooked with lures a web above our heads.
When it's over, we've caught our
limit and beyond, one of us has drowned,
and another's white calf's been taken
for a belly by a sand shark.
Next year we'll be back,
standing in the red sea with a wooden leg.

Boomers

We talk back and forth in dreams,
in the formic acid of the Web, wake
saying "run" and foam shoes soft
as mushrooms appear on store shelves,
say "quilt" and prices rise. Tolstoy said
we're ants, each hundred years things
waking in the dark of us to fight.
Our children were conceived in peace
but wear camouflage like jets, ball caps
like gun barrels. We were made in new
brick houses, between nightmares
in which our fathers flew like storks
over burning cities.

Theater

Like the neighborhood kind
you went to as a kid, full
of yellow light and red
velvet curtains and everybody
there, friends, bullies throwing
popcorn, somebody with red hair.
The roof is leak-stained like the bloody
footprints of the beast from 20,000 fathoms,
there's a yo-yo demonstration by
a greasy man in a sequined suit,
the girl you love is there somewhere
but you can't find her, or if you do
she's with some jerk with muscles.
And the show won't start. There's whistling
and stomping, paper airplanes and 3-D
glasses until you don't even care
anymore because your head is tired,
a stone atop a tendril, and you just
want to sleep, when, sure enough,
the curtain finally rises,
darkness falls,
and here it comes.

Reruns

My grandfather is in *The Maltese Falcon,* at least it looks like him. He's the hotel dick that Bogie gets to rough up Elisha Cook, Jr. I swear he could be Chester the way he wears his snap-brim hat on the side and talks out of the corner of his mouth. And Chester was a security guard, a rent-a-cop, after he quit being a butcher. I always watch that movie just for that part, just to see him young again, saying *G'won, scram.*

I just watched *King Kong* again too, and the same thing hit me. There's this scene where Robert Armstrong takes Fay Wray into a diner to get her something to eat because she's weak from hunger. Soon she'll be in the paw of a giant ape, but now she's grateful for the food and, later, her first job as a star. She's really gorgeous.

But what I noticed was the guy behind the bar who gives Armstrong a cup of coffee, then smiles at him for a second before the camera follows Armstrong away. I don't know what made me notice him; he's only on for a second. After the movie came out, he probably watched that scene a million times just to see himself in it. Maybe he didn't even know what the job was, just some B movie, a bit part, and he needed the money because it was the Depression. Then when he realized, I imagine him showing it over and over again to his kids and then to his grandkids, how granddaddy is on television again. Maybe they even made a point of watching it after he died.

He's a nice-looking man in a white waiter's jacket, and I bet he hands that coffee to Armstrong, somewhere in the world, a hundred times a day, and I guess he always will. It's odd to think of him in the earth, first sort of green, then yellow like old piano keys, then finally his skull brown and shiny like a fossil, even while he's handing over another cup and smiling one more time.

Litany in a Time of Drought

Only rain would make them call off
practice, or a coronary. I prayed all
first period, but in study hall
sun streamed in. Everyone chirped about
the string of beautiful days that lasted
from the third grade to the twelfth.
They hadn't heard why it was Hiroshima
that was bombed, its parks perfect
with sun, running with dogs and small lovers,
how rainy it was in Tokyo, how
enclosed they all were, reading in rooms
golden with lamplight, the murmur of rain
cracked once by thunder, far off.

Trying to be heroes, blocking
dummies was what we were, Robert Hand
and me, always bleeding somewhere, cut
grass and dust in noses, ears and hair.
We dreamed a machine, booth you step into,
get it over with, five minutes, free
by four fifteen, though that much pain at once
would kill—you have to spread
it out. We walked home in the dark, sure
there was no God.

Not that I don't pray.
When the sun brings out salesmen, bill
collectors, door-to-door evangelists,
B-52s, coaches and criminals,
I pray to the rain.

Chartres

This is a universe of broken symmetries.
—Einstein

I love winter because it made the world
into those black-and-white cowboy movies,
stripping every bush into sagebrush, uncovering
boulders and dirt trails that echoed my hooves
as I followed maps I'd stained and creased,
making all trees shadows, like those gnarled black olives
and California oranges, all grass brown prairie
grass. It has taken me forty years
to make this connection.

They burned Giordano Bruno for saying
the world was a stained glass picture
of God's mind, like the big one at Chartres,
and that we're born with the swept-up
shards a pile in our brain, spend our whole lives
piecing—the pale blue with the pale blue.
Some get a lot built, some a little, some
leave behind a part of this jigsaw, which is a saw
dancing a jig, not around things as they are
but through them as if to divide forever
the cowboy in the bottom left corner
from his black lariat twirling in the dead of winter.

Myth

Bluto loves Olive, so he kidnaps her,
her squeals like bird calls.
He rubs his pubic beard on her soft skin,
and his cigar stub is a fat penis.
He thinks she's beautiful with her
pot-handle hair.

She leaves a trail of breadcrumbs.

Once she's gone, snow starts falling
and the birds stop singing.
Maybe they miss her bird legs,
who knows?

When Popeye gets home from Paris,
the birds tell him Olive was taken,
that he should follow the crumbs they're hungry for.

So with a case of spinach and hornpipe
he follows her to Goon Island.

To make a long story short,
Popeye plays so badly that a two-headed
watchdog falls asleep, he beats up Bluto
and lots of goons, and he almost gets
Olive back home in time
for spring.

But at the last minute, just before the boat
lands, she looks back and turns
into salt.

Popeye's inconsolable
and never eats spinach again.

And that's why they sprinkle crumbs
of salt on the roads in winter,
and why they disappear.

The University of Hell

It's open admissions, free tuition, but Fs for everyone,
attendance is mandatory, and the classes seem eternal.
The pitchforks of the teaching assistants say no falling
asleep, no rest for the wicked, no soft answers
turning away wrath. They advance through the lower levels,
the core curriculum, each room packed and stifling—"Principles
of Envy" (prerequisite "Pride"), "Getting and Spending,"
"Advanced Rage." All old hat. The most popular courses
are "Escape Methods 101," and "History of Remorse."
Tired of the mill-stack smoke, the sinner-students try
to transfer—*Willing to Relocate,* they write,
but the flaming postman won't deliver, hands them
asbestos postcards: *If you're thinking of applying,*
don't. The restrooms are filthy, the graffiti
(*Satan Sucks*) never washed from the walls.
The elevators don't work—no one goes up anyway—
and not smoking is prohibited.

Everyone has tenure, even the students; they couldn't be fired
if they tried. The football program's well endowed, but except
when the Flies lose to the Angels once a millennium, the games
are intramural. There are no rules. The cheerleaders jump
and twitch and beat at their flaring skirts with blazing pompoms.
Howling the fight song "All Hope Abandon," the fans
in the stands in smoldering raccoon coats can hardly
see the players, silhouettes bashing each other
in the sulfurous light, trying to make the draft, though the big leagues
are full. Just as graduation is a cruel and empty ritual, the black wool
robes, the paper fans and programs catching fire, and then the walking
to applause across the stage to get that pre-signed, pre-approved entry
        form,
though all of them, even the *magma cum laude,* the Dishonor Students,
still have to stand in interminable lines, get the signature
of a smirking advisor, just to be freshmen all over again
because some people never learn.

Santa Anna's Leg, Obregón's Arm, and the Lungs of the Incas

Met with roses at the airport by other poets, musicians,
painters, we were embarrassed to know no Spanish.
At the bar hotel at night, a clean, well-lighted place,
with the waiters waiting to go home, we read Paz,
who'd just won the Nobel, we in translation,
they the originals with great rolling r's
that made us feel anemic, pallid. Eduardo sang
Puccini. *Wow,* someone said, *the lungs of the Incas.*
In La Fuente, the fountain, like the cantina
where Bogie and Tim Holt fight the bad boss
in *Treasure of the Sierra Madre,* we drank
margaritas, read more poetry, and someone
told about Santa Anna's rebel leg, lost
in battle, buried *azul* in unholy ground,
dug up and buried again when it changed
in the earth to the leg of *El Presidente,* then
dug up and dragged through the streets
in the *revolución.* He lost Texas, too,
so we drank to him with salt and sour limes.

Obregón's severed arm is said to have reached
for enemy legs on the battlefield, and Orozco
painted the priest Hidalgo's big fist hitting out
of the ceiling at the Spanish, and because it all
seemed to fit together like poetry, suddenly
I spoke of The Voice, *voz.* They thought I said
vos, us, but we liked the pun, our first
in Spanish, and drank another toast, *Chairs!*
to Señors Joyce and Finnegan.
In the square they were setting up
the crèche, golden sheep and shepherds,
and in the cathedral, with the altar to
Our Lady of Roses and the plaster body
of Christ under glass, his knee skin torn
to show the cap beneath, the Virgin
of Guadalajara was a doll's head riding
a fountain of blue dress to heaven.

Yearn

An only life can take so long to climb
Clear of its wrong beginnings, and may never.
      —"Aubade," Philip Larkin

A rare word with the year
in it, though it doesn't get
pronounced, unlike the *ought*
in *autumn* that, at your back,
you always hear. Though you do
hear the *urn,* or the *earn,*
which is not what you deserve, maybe,
or want, but just what you get,
like the truer blue
and deeper green of the shorter days,
the trees draining to their true colors,
which have been beautifully, though perhaps
uselessly, there all along, like the *year*
in *my earth* or *awfully early.*
Surely more poems have been written
about this season than any other,
poets being by nature—and that's where
they say they like to live—
morbid, which almost has *more*
in it, and certainly *orb.*
And *bid,* which is never high
enough, and is always right
before *goodbye.*

From
EVERYWHERE AT ONCE

University of Akron Press, 2008

Portrait of the Artist as a Young Boy

Waiting for the fight to start
when my father came home late again,
I'd drive my older sister nuts
as she tried to sleep in our shared bedroom
while I crooned to the dark "America
the Beautiful" or "The Marines' Hymn."
Get him out! she'd cry to my mother,
He's so weird!
So Mother tried reading to me,
stories, poems, and I'd sleep,
until the night she read Field's
"Little Boy Blue," how the little
toy soldier waited staunchly
in the attic for the little boy who died
to come back and play with him.
I cried so long and hard, she finally
had to put me in a cold bath
and give me hiccups.
After that, I made up my own songs,
my sister weeping every night as I sang
of a little toy soldier who ran
in the amber heaven of waves
of grain, or waited forever
in the hell of the empty halls
of Monty Zooma, or on the desolate
shores of Triple Lee.

Ophelia Writes Home

He passed so peacefully in sleep, it seemed
as in a kingly way, or in at least
what passes for a royal death in this
rough place where every bush may hide a bear.
He was a good provider, and we lived
if not as kings, then as two princes who
were born to make the best of baser things
and not forget how blessed we were to be
alive at all. It was Horatio,
you now can know, who hatched the plan to bate
the sword with sleeping potion, culled from stuff
he'd read at school in Wittenberg about
the young Italian lovers, feuding tribes,
a tomb for two. It just remained to bribe
the graveyard clowns to feign and shuttle both
the boxes (I no longer shivering
and wet) on board the pirate ship we dubbed
The Nunnery, a little jest which fed
the joy we felt in one another's arms
across the icy sea, until we reached
this Eden Danish men discovered past
the coldest land of all. Our children grew,
the crops rose tall, the swarthy neighbors brought
their harvest in to honor us at fall.
This is in secret—should you draw your breath
to tell his tale do not this letter show,
thereby his famous tragedy amending.
Recall his melancholy cast and know
how much he would abhor a happy ending.

Perseverance

My mother used to wear out belts
on my bony body, once broke
a Ouija board over my head,
and Daddy would sermonize till the cows
covered their ears, doctrine
off a duck's back. Schools only gave me
degrees to get me out, and girls got
so tired of saying *no* they married me.
Maybe perversity grows from a gene,
like grass through a sidewalk,
or hardens and mottles like a shell around
some soft psychic tissue till you have
an organ that plods on while the hares
are sleeping. And so as soon as Mother
would forbid me to go to the creek,
the dogs and I headed there like newts.
And when I finally went too far
that summer at the beach,
and the lifeguard had to bring me back in
to another whipping, I just kept grinning
at how far I'd gotten,
how many waves I'd broken
with my hard head.

The Audition

In this game we confess the things
about ourselves we've never told
before: Gary wearing the same shirt
for all four of his high school class pictures,
Jim doing something slightly shady
for the CIA in Nam, Kelly dancing topless
that summer to get through grad school.
I hesitate between the public swimming pool
when I was ten, or sitting on my brother's face
and breaking his nose, till I remember
Terry Mayo, not only the prettiest girl
in first grade, but maybe ever, so lovely
she was born for Frank Harris, who wore
a coat and tie to school, and, even I could see,
was handsome as a movie star. A little
sheepishly, I decide to scrawl on my scrap
of paper how, for her birthday, I gave her
a brown-plastic-framed picture
of Jesus, knowing my friends will laugh
for years to come. But what they won't know
is how she suddenly kissed me bang
on the mouth in the middle of the playground
in front of God and everybody, or that, when
Christmas came, it was not me, but Frank, gold
in the robe his mother made, who knelt
in the straw with the sheep, while I stood
next to her, cotton wool on my chin,
towel on my head, and felt
with my hand, for a full ten minutes,
her waist, tiny and warm.

The Side to the Wall

Considering this is the last Christmas tree
in Hattiesburg, Mississippi, it's not bad.
I recall all of the childhood lots, white
breath on the night air as gloved, rough men
held trees by the horns like trophies, stabbing
the stobs into the ground to show
how the needles, still fresh, stuck,
arguing the limbs would loosen, spread
like wings when left alone, given a good home.

But always the ribs of one side
stayed stove in from where it lay,
or were scraggled being dragged
from underneath the others.
We turned it to the wall, stinting
the lights and tinsel so as not to call
attention. Those limbs lived in shadow,
like the black of the moon, out
of reach, ungarnished, ungraced,
holding their dark like a slice of night,
below the awful angel that turned
its back and faced the light.

Just Man

*Then Joseph her husband, being a just man, and not willing to make
her a public example, was minded to put her away privately.*
— Matthew 1:19

Having a famous father-in-law
never helped him much, hurt,
really, the way his wife kowtowed:
His will be done.
And the story of the angel in the garden
must have been hard to swallow,
though he hoped his faith would
make him a savior in her eyes.
Instead, he was squeezed out first
of a honeymoon hotel, then
a barn by kneeling oxen, the stench
of shepherds, and strangers wearing turbans.
The gold was great, yes, but what
could you do with frankincense,
and what the hell was myrrh?
Admittedly, the child turned out
better than expected, never even cried,
even looked a little like him, happy
for hours playing in the sawdust pile.

But then, of course, everything went wrong
at the end, and she mourned so much
she never came to him again.
Still, he must have told himself, you don't
have to be happy, there's no *requirement,*
and so he learned the contentment
of the ordinary—sunrise, steam
of breakfast, smell of shavings and sweat
in the shop—the satisfaction
of doing small things well, sawing
studs, sanding the rough grain smooth,
nailing one piece of wood
across another.

Gross Anatomy

—after judging a poetry contest for medical students

It is difficult
to get the news from poems
yet men die miserably every day
for lack
of what is found there.
                                              —William Carlos Williams

Half their poems are sick from watching,
for the first time, someone die, pale
and helpless amid the drone and drip

of machines, and the rest suffer
the thing itself, the empty hands, blue
as Dührer's, into which they place again,

in their minds and on paper, the toys,
roses, and other hands they once held.
But though they saw open the skull,

raise the pate on its waste-bin hinge,
lift out the brain, and stare into the bowl
where they imagine memories still float

like petals on dark water, and though they
"crack" the chest with a melon sound, lift
and weigh the liver and lights, and hold

in their hands the heavy heart,
it's the shrunken sex and withered breasts
that prove too much for ones so young

and impel them to try and tell, witness
to what they have seen. And so they write
it down, send it off, then wait to hear

that it has won, for how can it miss
since it really happened, even the names—
embolism, arteriovenus, curettage—pure poetry.

Canterbury Tale

The flowers she buys at the grocery
spray from a jam jar, though we
can afford crystal now.
When in April, twenty years ago,
on a campus sidewalk, stopped
by a glance of sunlight on a bell tower,
she exclaimed, *How like this is
to Canterbury*—but pronounced it
canta-bree—I, Georgia cracker, frustrated
Anglo-, Italo-, Francophile,
was stunned, struck down by love, like
Dante by Beatrice, by her whiff
of cucumber sandwiches and tea cakes,
her skin like gold museum glint
on gesso, her legs of pink
Carrara marble, and her Jamesian claim
that American men were inferior
to European. So I scratched
my shaggy skull for foreign words,
took up opera, told her
I wrote poetry.

Turns out, she was from
Mississippi, and, Reader,
I married her—the salt lick
of her, the swish
of ceiling fans, afternoon
pinking the pillars of cloud
over the Gulf, gouache
of gumbo, pentimento
of peppery boiled crabs,
all washed down by
sweet tea in a jam jar.

The Others

Come away, O human child!
To the waters and the wild
With a faery, hand in hand...
—"The Stolen Child," W. B. Yeats

Did he climb this barren
height alone,
lost on his way home
as twilight came
and went?
Searchers never thought
to look up here,
this terrible steep
where the only sounds
are the bawls of sheep
and the wind's sheepdog whistle.
Tommy Jones, five years old,
it says on the stone
that silhouettes this ridge
a thousand feet above his farm
and peers down into
the lonely lap of a faery
pool, bottomless, the locals say,
though its clear, green surface
shimmers, riffles, mirrors
whatever the changeling
shapes of wind and clouds
and light might want,
will have.

Twice Removed

France has been, as the guidebooks say,
enchanting, the Pyrenees frosted with snow,
and the food! Creamy sauces and snails.
But after a week, we're homesick, though
for America, where we live, or Wales,
where we're living this hopscotch year,
we don't know. *Home* is many-layered
as an onion, and none can make us weep
anymore. *Hiraeth,* the Welsh call that
inconsolable longing for place,
but we long for too many.
I like the way the Plains Indians just
rolled up their houses and rode away,
took their few possessions and all
the people they knew with them.
What Mother couldn't move in a day,
the IRS got. What did they do, I wonder,
with my high school yearbook, all those
young faces stratified in the dark
of some warehouse somewhere?
If I could see even one of my graduating
class, I'd know how old I was,
but they're as scattered
as I. How do we put the heart
back in hearth? One *pied* in air,
we need another in some *terre*
besides the grave.
I still dream about my first house.
Now that was a home.
Where I fell on the floor furnace
that burned a chessboard on my knee.
Scarred and waiting for my next move,
look: it's still there, always will be.

Acknowledgments

Pressure Under Grace. Breitenbush Books, 1982.

"The Fortune." *Ellipsis* 6.1 (1978): 53.

"Heir Apparent." *Wind* 2.42 (1981): 17.

"My Father's House." *Family Matters: Poems of Our Families.* Ann Smith and Larry Smith, eds. Bottom Dog Press, 2005: 150.

"The House on the Second Floor." *CEA Forum* 21.2 (Summer 1991): 7-8.

Where We've Been. Breitenbush Books, 1987.

"Heart." *Poetry* 142.2 (May 1983): 86.

"The Unities on North Avenue." *The Laurel Review* 19.2 (Summer 1985): 18.

"Double Feature." *South Florida Poetry Review* 4.1 (Fall 1986): 16.

"The Life of the Mind." *Negative Capability* 3.1 (Winter 1982): 57.

"Men as Trees, Walking." *The Valley Beneath Words: The Best of Plainsong.* Bowling Green, Kentucky: Plainsong Press, 1995: 20.

"Men as Trees, Walking." *Quiet Music: A Plainsong Reader.* Bowling Green, Kentucky: Plainsong Press, 1995: 19.

"Milledgeville." *New Virginia Review* 4 (1986): 84.

"A1A." *South Florida Poetry Review* 4.1 (Fall 1986): 17.

"Pit Pony." *Western Ohio Journal* 11.1 (Spring 1990): 108.

"A Cat in Eden." *Piedmont Literary Review* 9.2 (Summer 1984): n. pag.

"Karma." *Piedmont Literary Review* 9.2 (Summer 1984): n. pag.

"Visitation." *Seattle Review* 7.1 (Spring 1984): 53.

"The Weaning." *Poetry* 142.2 (May 1983): 85.

"It's What You Said You Wanted." *Western Ohio Journal* 11.1 (Spring 1990): 19.

"Nothing's Been the Same Since John Wayne Died." *Plainsong* 6.1 (Winter 1985): 45.

"Our Father Who Art on Third." *South Florida Poetry Review* 4.1 (Fall 1986): 73.

How the Dead Bury the Dead. University of Akron Press, 1994.

"How the Dead Bury the Dead." *American Poetry Review* 21.1 (Jan./Feb. 1992): 6.

"Yards." *Prairie Schooner* 63.4 (Winter 1989): 24.

"Hardheads." *Poetry Northwest* 33.4 (Winter 1992-93): 11.

"Anniversary." *Poetry* 161.5 (February 1993): 257.

"Hands." *Poet & Critic* 25.2 (Winter 1994): 29.

"Tying a Tie." *New Virginia Review* 8 (1991): 20.

"First Love." *Slant* 5 (Summer 1991): 42.

"Small Road to Nowhere." *Poetry* 152.3 (June 1988): 130.

"Bayou." *Southern Poetry Review* 34.2 (Winter 1994): 45-46.

"Skin." *Xavier Review* 13.1 (Spring 1993): 52.

"Advent." *Oxford Magazine* 3.2 (Fall/Winter 1987): 59.

"Rust Belt." *Pig Iron* 16 (1990): 52.

"The Original Adam and Eve." *The Laurel Review* 25.1 (Winter 1991): 13.

"Seventh Heaven." *Poetry* 163.3 (December 1993): 156.

"Tool." *Piedmont Literary Review* 14.4: 22.

"Tenderhooks." *Poetry Northwest* 35.1 (Spring 1994): 44-45.

"All of Us Are Children." *The Laurel Review* 25.1 (Winter 1991): 12.

"The History of Effects." *Writer's Almanac,* November 28, 2008.

"Hypochondria." *Poetry* 159.1 (October 1991): 14.

"Entrance." *Poetry* 152.3 (June 1988): 129.

Simmer Dim. University of Akron Press, 1999.

"Blodeuwedd." *New Welsh Review* 37: 22.

"At Arthur's Stone." *New Welsh Review* 37: 23.

"Footpaths." *Missouri Review* 20.1 (1997): 110.

"Bread of Heaven." *Poem* 74 (November 1995): 49.

"Welsh Courier Braves Daylight." *Nimrod* 41.2 (Spring/Summer 1998): 115.

"The Silkie." *The Southern Review* 33.2 (Spring 1997): 254.

"Hooks." *New Welsh Review* 31 (Winter 1995-96): 27.

Ascending Order. University of Akron Press, 2003.

"A Woman Brought to Child." *Snapdragon* 10:1&2 (Winter 1987): 61.

"Them." *Poetry* 163.4 (January 1994): 202.

"Cupidity." *Planet: The Welsh Internationalist* 147 (June/July 2001): 14.

"Running the Body." *Poetry* 179 (December 2001): 147.

"The Poet, Calling the Kettle Black." *Poetry Northwest* 40.2 (Summer 1999): 25.

"Priscilla." *Planet: The Welsh Internationalist* 138 (December 1999/January 2000): 33.

"First Impression." *Incliner* 10 (2002).

"Prostrate." *The Southern Review* 36.4 (Autumn 2000): 747.

Fishing at the End of the World, Word Press, 2005.

"Silly Mid-Off." *The Ledge Magazine* 27 (Winter/Spring 2003-2004): 91.

"Waiting Rooms." *Onionhead* (Winter 1989): 26.

"Mary Faye." *Fine Madness* 6.1 (Spring/Summer 1989): 28.

"It's My Karma, and I'll Cry if I Want To." *The Laurel Review* 34.1 (Winter 2000): 61.

"Finally." *Fine Madness* 6.1 (Spring/Summer 1989): 26.

"Fishing at the End of the World" (as "Cabesa de Lobo"). *Louisiana Literature* (Fall 1989): 48.

"Boomers." *Poetry* 152.3 (June 1988): 129.

"Theater." *Spoon River Quarterly* 14.1 (Winter 1989): 14.

"Reruns." *Movieworks.* Rochester, New York: Little Theatre Press, 1990: 128.

"Litany in a Time of Drought." *Aethlon: The Magazine of Sport Literature* 6.2 (Spring 1989): 78.

"Chartres." *The Little Magazine* 17 (1991): 77.

"Myth." *California State Poetry Quarterly* 23.3 (Spring 1997): 44.

"The University of Hell." *88: A Journal of Contemporary American Poetry* 1 (December 2001): 46.

"Santa Anna's Leg, Obregón's Arm, and the Lungs of the Incas." *Gadfly* (Spring 1991): 43.

"Yearn." *Poetry* 166.3 (June 1995): 164.

Everywhere at Once, University of Akron Press, 2008

"Portrait of the Artist as a Young Boy." *Louisiana Literature* 24.1 (Spring/Summer): 24.

"Ophelia Writes Home." *Mississippi Review* 29.3 (Summer 2001): 136.

"Perseverance." *Prairie Schooner* 81.2 (Summer 2007): 110.

"The Audition." *America* 191.20 (December 20-27, 2004): 19.

"The Side to the Wall." *The Southern Review* 40.4 (Autumn 2004): 641.

"Just Man." *Artful Dodge* 48/49: 54.

"Gross Anatomy" (as "The Autopsy Poems"). *Poetry Wales* 40.3 (2004/5): 43.

"Canterbury Tale." *The Southern Review* 40.4 (Autumn 2004): 640-41.

"Twice Removed." *Twice Removed,* Main Street Rag Chapbook Series, 2006.

"The Others." *Twice Removed,* Main Street Rag Chapbook Series, 2006.

Cover art, "Muszelki (Sea Shells, Sanibel Island)" by Maha Rashi; author photo by Mindi Greenway; cover and interior book design by Diane Kistner (dkistner@futurecycle.org); Gentium Book Basic text with Cronos Pro titling

About FutureCycle Press

FutureCycle Press is dedicated to publishing lasting English-language poetry books, chapbooks, and anthologies in both print-on-demand and ebook formats. Founded in 2007 by long-time independent editor/publishers and partners Diane Kistner and Robert S. King, the press incorporated as a nonprofit in 2012. A number of our editors are distinguished poets and writers in their own right, and we have been actively involved in the small press movement going back to the early seventies.

The FutureCycle Poetry Book Prize and honorarium is awarded annually for the best full-length volume of poetry we publish in a calendar year. Introduced in 2013, our Good Works projects are anthologies devoted to issues of universal significance, with all proceeds donated to a related worthy cause. Our Selected Poems series highlights contemporary poets with a substantial body of work to their credit; with this series we strive to resurrect work that has had limited distribution and is now out of print. We are dedicated to giving all of the authors we publish the care their work deserves, making our catalog of titles the most diverse and distinguished it can be, and paying forward any earnings to fund more great books.

We've learned a few things about independent publishing over the years. We've also evolved a unique, resilient publishing model that allows us to focus mainly on vetting and preserving for posterity the most books of exceptional quality without becoming overwhelmed with bookkeeping and mailing, fundraising activities, or taxing editorial and production "bubbles." To find out more about what we are doing, come see us at www.futurecycle.org.

The FutureCycle Poetry Book Prize

All full-length volumes of poetry published by FutureCycle Press in a given calendar year are considered for the annual FutureCycle Poetry Book Prize. This allows us to consider each submission based on its own merits, outside of the context of a contest. Too, the judges see the finished book, which will have benefitted from the beautiful book design and strong editorial gloss we are famous for.

The book ranked the best in judging is announced as the prize-winner in the subsequent year. There is no fixed monetary award; instead, the winning poet receives an honorarium of 20% of the total net royalties from all poetry books and chapbooks the press sold online in the year the winning book was published. The winner is also accorded the honor of being on the panel of judges for the next year's competition and, in this capacity, receives a copy of all books in contention for that year's prize.